MW00973805

The Process of Fulfillment

Workbook

Get Out of the Way

This exercise is an exercise in paying attention to what's holding you back. Most of the time, the biggest obstacle to our own destiny is ourselves. You must practice getting out of your own way. A clue into this strategy is to simply pay attention to what you pay attention to. Sometimes you can subconsciously focus on things that are not necessary for accomplishment. Your focus is a choice to hold on to something that takes up too much mental real estate. There are many things in life that weigh you down and block your ability to be fully mobile in life and live with a sense of fulfillment, accomplishment, peace, and happiness. I call these weights or "bricks". We pack these bricks in our luggage of life as we travel along life's journey. When you reach a stressful point in your life or you find it difficult to move ahead in life, you must then stop and pay attention to your life. Move those things out of the way that are blocking your success. This is a crucial and vital step to help you accomplish greatness.

When you hold on to "stuff", it is a personal choice. You spend more time fixing issues than building your dreams. When you focus on fixing your issues, you build a deeper relationship to those issues and carry those issues as weighted bricks. It is here where you can begin the process of identifying the bricks that you might have packed in your luggage. Yes! Life happens. Things happen to us all the time that are beyond our control, but you and I are fully responsible for what things we hold on to and what things we let go of. You must get out of your own way. Most people do not realize that they are carrying huge amounts of baggage or luggage full of bricks. Some are never taught to stop and take inventory of what they are carrying. So...

1. Do not fix. Refocus on your greatness.

Today when you fly on most airlines, baggage fees are attached to the price of the ticket. This forces most people to become conscious of how much they are packing into their luggage. Literally, you can put your bag on the scale at the check-in counter, and because you have too much in a piece of luggage, you can pay as much as $50.00 more. With this, people become mindful of the amount of stuff packed in their luggage simply because they are mindful of the extra cost. So...

2. Be mindful of life's extra cost.

You have to realize that there is always an extra cost for extra baggage and overweight luggage. If you are aware of the cost, you would most likely pay more attention to the luggage and what's in it.

If you feel that you are in some way losing in life, I want you to transfer the concept of losing to the concept of paying a higher price. What's causing you to lose? What's causing you to pay a higher price? It can simply be how you see things, how you evaluate things, and the how you process things. You might experience what's in front of you as a loss, but on the other side, you are actually exchanging energy with what you are facing or wrestling with. Energy is just like money. It carries the same characteristics of flow and exchange. When you are losing energy, you are paying out an extra price for extra luggage. What you focus on, is your point of exchange of your personal energy, and most times one does not know that they are paying a high life price because they are unconscious of their focus, unconscious of what's in their bags, and unconscious of the price they are paying. So...

3. Check your luggage.

Here we will identify three types of luggage that can be loaded with bricks:

A. Childhood Luggage   **B. Circumstantial Luggage**   **C. Relationship Luggage**

I want to be clear here. You do not need to be on a psychologist's couch to figure this stuff out. You must take responsibility for bettering your own life. Life does not happen to you, life happens from you. Most people are aware and have knowledge of most of their issues. You are fully responsible for both the issues that you know about, in addition to the ones that you may ignore and not be conscious of. You must begin the process of emptying yourself for clarity of direction.

Bringing issues from the unconscious to the conscious is a matter of self-reflection and asking yourself to allow what might be buried deep within you to be revealed. You are an intelligent being and you are not at the mercy of any device that is beyond your control to resolve. You must be serious about reflecting on your personal history as well as the present, and you must be totally honest with yourself.

You have enough people in the world that are more than ready to cheat you out of your personal energy or "psychological money". So please don't cheat yourself. Be prepared to be fully honest and fully reflective for this exercise to work.

Now we are going to make some challenging lists.

Step 1

Make a list of every possible thing you think is wrong in your life:

1. _____
2. _____
3. _____
4. _____
5. _____
6. _____
7. _____
8. _____
9. _____
10. _____

Step 2

Get the opinion of someone you know that loves you. It can be a parent, sibling, pastor, mentor, or guidance counselor. Make sure it is someone who has observed you and can be honest with you. Have them to list out things they observe about you that can be better:

1. _____
2. _____
3. _____
4. _____
5. _____
6. _____
7. _____
8. _____
9. _____
10. _____

Step 3

List things that you do not quite like (personally) about yourself, and the things in your life that can be improved upon. Be complete. Be thorough:

1. _____
2. _____
3. _____
4. _____
5. _____
6. _____
7. _____
8. _____
9. _____
10. _____

Step 4

List the things in your life that you feel are missing. It can be people, or it can be physical things.

1. _____
2. _____
3. _____
4. _____
5. _____
6. _____
7. _____
8. _____
9. _____
10. _____

Write the following statement and repeat it to yourself:

I AM responsible for all of this!

The key is, as we work on these lists, you will continue to repeat this statement until everything on these lists is unpacked from your luggage.

You are the creator and designer for everything in your life. You are the chooser. You pack your luggage. Yes. Often, things happen to you that you had no responsibility or voluntary involvement, but the "happening" does not start there. That's why I can say, strangely enough, nothing happened to you at these points. "Happenings" only happen when you exchange your energy with what's in front of you. How do you connect to what you think? You block yourself when you get too involved with past circumstances that add no value to where you are going. That's why you must be careful not to block your own way via your choices.

When you choose to engage what's in front of you, that's when "what happens" begins. So nothing "happens" until you engage and exchange your energy. This is what gives any situation or circumstance definition, and all definitions come personally from you. If you are the definer, then you are the designer. This is why life is fully your response-ability or your ability to respond. Human beings are "responders". We are not animals with auto-responses that are built in. You can design each and every one of your responses, even in the worst of circumstances.

What's beautiful about this is that even though a good number of your over-packed luggage comes from your childhood experiences and your responses to those experiences; you can redesign and re-respond to every one of those childhood traumas or beliefs. You can reposition yourself for greatness! The human mind is amazing.

You can Re-Respond to any past incident that you have already responded to in different way

Step 5

On the next page, give each item a short name. If you can put a date on it please do so. ***Please, never be general in your answers. Be very specific.*** For example:

1. I lost my job when I was working at ABC Company.

Short version:

1. Job loss ABC Company (December 2013)

2. I was molested as a child by my mom's coworker.

Short version:

2. Molested by George (Age 6)

3. I am missing the right relationship in my life. I need a good mate.

Short version:

3. Missing a mate. I need sex. (Current)

Put all of these in the first column. In the second column identify the type of luggage this may be.

A. Childhood Luggage	B. Circumstantial Luggage	C. Relationship Luggage
1. Job loss (December 2013)		Circumstantial Luggage
2. Molested (Age 6)		Childhood Luggage
3. Missing a mate (Current)		Relationship Luggage

There is no right or wrong answer. Be open and honest with yourself. Be complete to the best of your ability. This is just a starting point. You might have to make adjustments, but rest assure as you clear some of these items from your luggage, more will show up and present themselves to be resolved.

Shortened Version   **Type of Luggage**

1.   _____   _____
2.   _____   _____
3.   _____   _____
4.   _____   _____
5.   _____   _____
6.   _____   _____
7.   _____   _____
8.   _____   _____
9.   _____   _____
10. _____   _____
11. _____   _____
12. _____   _____
13. _____   _____
14. _____   _____
15. _____   _____
16. _____   _____
17. _____   _____
18. _____   _____
19. _____   _____
20. _____   _____
21. _____   _____
22. _____   _____
23. _____   _____
24. _____   _____
25. _____   _____
26. _____   _____
27. _____   _____
28. _____   _____
29. _____   _____
30. _____   _____
31. _____   _____
32. _____   _____
33. _____   _____
34. _____   _____
35. _____   _____
36. _____   _____
37. _____   _____
38. _____   _____
39. _____   _____
40. _____   _____

Repack your luggage in the correct category. Whatever you identified for each item, place that item in the correct category. Use the short name:

A. Childhood Luggage   **B. Circumstantial Luggage**   **C. Relationship Luggage**

A. Childhood Luggage	B. Circumstantial Luggage	C. Relationship Luggage
_____	_____	_____
_____	_____	_____
_____	_____	_____
_____	_____	_____
_____	_____	_____
_____	_____	_____
_____	_____	_____
_____	_____	_____
_____	_____	_____
_____	_____	_____
_____	_____	_____
_____	_____	_____
_____	_____	_____
_____	_____	_____
_____	_____	_____
_____	_____	_____
_____	_____	_____

What you will find is that some of you will have more relationship baggage. Some will be dealing primarily with handling negative circumstances, and some will have extensive childhood issues. Some may have a balance of all three. The idea is to get to know what kind they are and where they come from.

Here is the good news about all of these items. As time passes, you develop nuero-pathways that further embed these relationships or energy exchanges into your life. This makes this a science and thusly you can use scientific and measurable processes to deal with them.

Now each item resembles a brick or a weight in your luggage. You can continue to carry these bricks in your luggage or you can use these same bricks to build a foundation. Nothing about a foundation for a house is pretty or appealing. It's not supposed to be. Nothing about these instances in your life is pretty or enjoyable, but they are needed for a foundation. So we will begin the process of transferring these bricks from your luggage for foundational use!

Your list is no longer a list of horrors, but the beginning to a new and exciting life. So let's write this and make it a part of your new and modified belief system.

My list is no longer a list of horrors, but the beginning to a new and exciting life!

_____
_____
_____
_____
_____
_____
_____
_____
_____

Write it a few times and say it many times over. Now let's secure your passport to your most exciting journey.

Notes:

Choosing Into Your Best Life

What exist before you is like a blank canvas, but you cannot observe a blank canvas without getting out your own way with thoughts that interrupt your own destiny. Although you see things and circumstances, and although you have experiences, life remains empty and waiting for it to be created. Choices give us this emptiness. We have many choices to make. Where can I go? What can I see? How can this or that be created? What do I do next? Who shall I be with? Because of choice, you can easily consider any life before you as a blank canvas. Yes. Although situation A, B, or C has happened, the fact that you have the power to redirect your mind renders any future that stands before you a blank canvas. Current conditions are never final because choice always remains.

Some people are stuck in a limiting belief like, "I don't have enough money." This, like many others, is a limiting belief because it assumes that an outside source dictates our life. If you do not have money for example, choice gives you the basis to find a way to receive or make money. You can choose out of anything that you have experienced, but there must be a willingness to let go of what's not serving you. You are the only one that personally chose to hold on to what doesn't serve you. That's why it is vital to get out of your own way. It is about being resourceful and determining a way to simply just make it happen. It is our limiting beliefs that get in the way of us doing things we desire or wish to do. Choice keeps any circumstance from becoming a finality. If things are not working as efficiently as you would like, choose beyond your current views.

Your limiting beliefs of the world or things you have determined as your 'truths' can get in the way of your choices. You are bombarded with many outside influences that help to determine who you are; however, you can choose to be one of those influences. You can choose what influences you. Influence can, at times, be so strong, you can be left with the feeling that there are no choices or limited choices. But here, you would need to consider yourself as being your own influence. Never take yourself out of the equation.

Often we look to things that we have no control over to fog our ability to choose our own life. Even when everything feels like it is totally and utterly out of your control or it appears that everyone and everything else has control over your life and you cannot do anything about it; get this, you still have control. In fact, in life, no matter what you encounter you have control over three things: what you think, what you say, and what you do. You are constantly making choices in these three areas. First you choose what you think about and what you focus on. Secondly, you choose the words you speak and how you choose to speak them. Lastly, you choose how you can respond in your life or react.

Here are three sets of things to remember:

1. **You can choose what you think about and focus on.**

2. **You can choose the words you speak and how you speak them.**

3. **You can choose how you respond to your life and react.**

1. You can choose what influences you.

2. You can choose to be your own influence.

3. You can choose your outcomes.

1. **You have control over what you what we think.**

2. **You have control over what you say.**

3. **You have control over what you do.**

1. In every moment you are making a decision.

2. In every moment you are focused on something.

3. In every moment your energy follows your focus.

With all of this:

It's all about choices! You control the choices. Choice directs your emotion. Emotion directs your energy.

Energy = Psychological Money

Your emotions are the launch-pad for your thoughts. So let's see how much your bags weigh and put a price on it! You might be spending too much of your life resources.

Step 1

Relist the bricks in your luggage and we are going to attach an energy price point to each. Each energy point represents the price tag on that event and you have to determine if you want to keep spending the energy. Keep your answers short. Don't try to tell a story! Every story becomes your life. You are only interested in a one-line short response.

Childhood Bricks   **What has been your response? (Action/Event Oriented)**

_____   _____

_____   _____

_____   _____

_____   _____

_____   _____

_____   _____

_____   _____

_____   _____

_____   _____

Example:

My father always called me dumb   I cover it by calling people dumb or my own children dumb

Circumstantial Bricks **What has been your response?**

_____   _____
_____   _____
_____   _____
_____   _____
_____   _____
_____   _____
_____   _____
_____   _____
_____   _____

Example:

I am depressed (Answer not good)

Going home depresses me (Better)   I take a strong drink when I get home.

Relationship Bricks	What has been your response?
_____	_____
_____	_____
_____	_____
_____	_____
_____	_____
_____	_____
_____	_____
_____	_____
_____	_____
My dad doesn't like me	I look for love through many other men

Remember, every response involves what you think, what you say, and what you do. You are solely responsible for everything. All of these things that you have full control over build a chemical set into your body called emotions. Emotions determine your energy or what you are spending on the luggage. It becomes the price you pay!

What you want to do is change the price on each item by reducing the weight of each item. You do this by changing your response. When you change your response, the brick becomes a foundation instead of being a weight. Any response that feels bad or dark is not the right response and is too heavy. When you change your response, you change what's costing you.

Let me underline the importance of this. As I said before, this is a matter of science and not happenstance. Nothing happens until it happens inside you. Nothing happens until you engage whatever is in front of you, and then you process it internally. This process scientifically turns into chemicals within your body. Your body always creates the chemicals to match your choices. Once these chemicals are in place, they have vibratory properties called frequencies. These frequencies inside your body entrain frequencies outside of your body, thusly creating more of the same situations.

When you relate to any circumstance, you set a frequency based on your response. This frequency then relates to everything around it that's like it. Some say that this is the law of attraction, but what it really is, is just you tuning into what's already there. You do not attract the negative, you turn into the negative and what's there that's negative becomes available to you. So when you feel sorry for yourself about something you don't like or something that happened to you, that feeling is aligning with a host of other energies and relationships that's unimaginable. So you must change the value of your responses!

Step 2

Let's change the value of all the responses. First, all your responses boil down to one common belief:

You are not enough.

A. Go back and take a black marker, and in the first columns of each luggage type, mark over every brick until you can't see the brick. Keep the responses!
B. Now read each response and repeat the words "I am not enough" after each.

Now do you see and understand how it all starts with a literal value? We respond to things based on the value we place on ourselves and not what happens to us. Take response-ability.

Step 3

A. Go back to Step 6 in the luggage chapter and get your bricks again.

B. This time start your response with I am enough. You cannot just say this one time. You have to say it until you feel it. If need be, get a trusted friend and have them to tell you that you are enough. That's it. Say it until you feel it. This is the turn. Say it until you feel it. If you are sitting down, stand up. Say it until you feel it.

You already know it. Trust me; your body is designed to believe you. Just keep saying it. Your body will soon create the chemicals. At this point, it becomes a matter of science. So when you feel it, listen to what your mind tells you then. Write down what your new responses are and will be.

Childhood Bricks   **What is your new response?**

_____   _____

_____   _____

_____   _____

_____   _____

_____   _____

_____   _____

_____   _____

_____   _____

_____   _____

Example:

My father always called me dumb   I am enough. I will spend time educating people on self- value.

Here the father can only call out to the child what he thinks about himself. So he needs the education also. So the response is to educate.

Circumstantial Bricks   **What is your new response?**

_____   _____

_____   _____

_____   _____

_____   _____

_____   _____

_____   _____

_____   _____

_____   _____

_____   _____

Example:

Going home depresses me   I am enough. I will clean up. I will bring the fun when I show up!

Relationship Bricks	What is your new response?
_____	_____
_____	_____
_____	_____
_____	_____
_____	_____
_____	_____
_____	_____
_____	_____
_____	_____
My dad doesn't like me	I am enough. I will focus on who does like me and build around that.

What's exciting about this whole process is that it is never too late to change your response to an event. Here are some more helpful tips:

1. **Become mindful of your thoughts.**

2. **Your decisions shape your life.**

3. **Your words reflect your value. So say the right thing until you feel it. Then act.**

4. **Your emotions are chemicals. You create them. They do not create you.**

Your responses carry value. You determine those values. You are your own destination. Your responses are your passport to the destination called "You".

Making It Easy to Stay Out of Your Own Way

There's a profound process, in terms of positioning yourself, that leads to your greatness. It includes letting go of your thought processes and taking in the initial strategy below by adding people in your life that can help you maintain the energy of your direction. Here are 3 types of effective persons that you need to maintain right energy;

1. Mentor
2. Like-Minded
3. Supportive

- The majority of learning, which is invested into your potential greatness, comes from those who are greatly accomplished. This precedes your own accomplishment. Anything that's a part of anyone's greatness extends from other people. Submit to learning from others. Get a mentor or mentors.

List 5 things you are attempting to accomplish:

1. _____
2. _____
3. _____
4. _____
5. _____

Next, list 5 people, whether you know them personally or not, that has accomplished what you are attempting to accomplish.

1. _____
2. _____
3. _____
4. _____
5. _____

Make a point to contact these people to create a relationship so you can model their activities. If the person is a professional and you cannot maintain consistent communication; buy their books, audio programs, or attend their online events. The key is to model their efforts, which helps you to maintain new focus and not slip back into being in your own way.

- Let go enough to involve others. Every great accomplishment was intertwined with others who were capable of contributing a piece of their own greatness. Leave space to work and interact with others. Exchange is the basis of all types of economy. You must position yourself to have masterful exchanges. This is classic "team-building".

It is said that 33% of your time must be spent with those who are doing what you are doing. These are not necessarily mentors, but those who are in the same field you are in, those who have similar goals you have and are practicing moving towards those goals, and then those who are in the same business you are in. This helps to keep your conversations and activities on an energy level that will serve you versus take away from one. One of the keys to maintaining the place where you separate yourself from the luggage you hold onto is to spend time with persons in this category.

Make a list of people that are in the field you are in, those who have similar goals, and those who are in a similar business you are in.

1. _____
2. _____
3. _____
4. _____
5. _____
6. _____
7. _____
8. _____
9. _____
10. _____

More importantly, list 10 people that you are currently involved with or close to. Include family.

1. _____
2. _____
3. _____
4. _____
5. _____
6. _____
7. _____
8. _____
9. _____
10. _____

How many in your second list qualify or show up in your first list. Now you need to shift the balance of your conversations and interactions. Make sure a majority of your time with persons in your first list.

- Empty yourself enough to be exposed to the energy that others can offer you. Your personal relationships are a great source of energy. This energy must be managed. Bad energy will rob you of the vitality needed to complete your tasks. There are, however, those who are capable depositing great energy. Do not close yourself off from these people.

This you involves your relationships that are close and intimate. It generally involves those who are capable of supporting you and your direction. Not everyone around you has a concern for what you want to accomplish. You must identify those that do. The key word here is "support". You can be entirely surprised at the level of support that you don't having although you might be surrounded by many people or actively engaged with people. You must monitor this.

Who supports you?

1. _____
2. _____
3. _____
4. _____
5. _____

Whether intentional or unintentional, who are those that you are actively involved with that do not offer support for your goals or direction?

1. _____
2. _____
3. _____
4. _____
5. _____

This second list is ultimately more important than the first. The second list is purely about the loss of energy. This means you have a relationship that exists in your mind one way, but plays out in your life another way. You should not have a second list. I cannot over express this. Supportive relationships should be 100% and not 33%. You will want to ask persons that make the second list to join the first list or you must cut them out or stop involvement and communication. You do not want to start anything at a loss.

The energy of non-support causes you to be awake only to the energy of the things you don't want in life. To lighten the load of things that cost you in life, you must maintain energy tie-ins that drive you to the top of your game.

These three points position you to intake information that comes from your own intelligence and brilliance. This intelligence and brilliance, I will call your light, much like a light bulb of an idea that pops in your head, but this light also comes with complete instruction towards your accomplishment. Moreover, there are so many other energetic processes, which come into play, that drive your greatness and accomplishment.

Positioning Yourself for Real Change

I want to use as an example, a person who has booked a flight to their favorite destination. I truly feel there is a distinct line between people who want to travel and people who want to travel but don't. The distinct line is the departure. I feel that there is always a reason not to go. Some people think it is money or time, others think it is their job, family or current situation. There are many reasons not to travel; however, the people who do travel tend to seek out the reasons to take that leap and make that move. In order to get to your destination you must make a move.

Most times we are thrilled to get out of where we are, jump into the excitement of visiting a new place, and experiencing a different way of life. Yet, right at the point of departure, everything you really like about where you are will tend to be magnified. It's as though it is a test to determine how much you really want to experience something new. The going is not the difficult part, the leaving is.

The going is not the difficult part, the leaving is.

Hopefully you are excited about moving towards higher heights.

Quick Tip:

Surround yourself with people who are where you want to be! Make sure you complete the exercise and act on the exercise of placement three types of persons in your environment; your mentor, your friends or business partners who are doing what you do, and people who support you.

Moving on can be difficult. Changing your response to an issue can be scary? Why? Even though the responses listed in the Luggage part of this workbook are not healthy, they can be comfortable to you. What's comfortable about something that's hurting you? This is what I mean by standing away. There is a tendency to hold on to things that does not work for you. You must position yourself to release these things. Otherwise it can become highly difficult to move forward.

There are two components of traveling, planning a vacation, or moving forward to a new destination. One is where you have decided to go. The other component is something few people are rarely conscious of, and that's where and what you are leaving. A lot of times fear is not generated because of what you want to accomplish, fear is generated because of where you have to leave or what you have to leave in order to accomplish what you want. This is why I listed the three areas in which we carry baggage.

A. Childhood   **B. Circumstantial**   **C. Relationship**

1. Most people do not want to grow up and mature past the past...leave the past
2. Most people don't want to change their circumstances; they want to bring their old circumstance into their new venture.
3. Most people don't want to leave the familiar faces of old and useless friends and family.

If you want to visit the Virgin Islands, can you pull the Virgin Islands over to the United States? No. You must board a plane and fly over, or swim over if you can. Either way, it involves leaving something. People make changes without changing and then find that nothing has changed.

For every response you create that's new, you must make a change or depart from an old place to accompany your new decision.

    A.   **You must grow past or mature past old issues.**
    B.   **You must change your surroundings.**
    C.   **You must change the relationships that are tied to what's old.**

Throw this workbook away if you're not willing to do any of these three. There is no reason to buy an expensive ticket to go somewhere and can't leave behind something in order to get where you are going. Get out of your own way.

You know about the signs that have all the items you must leave if you want to board an airplane. You are no longer dealing with just the bricks that are costing you more for your trips, but you are dealing with items that will keep you from moving forward. These are actual commitments to yourself of letting go or making changes, and without talking to a psychiatrist or any other type of professional, you know what these things are. You have to leave them behind.

What is your point of focus? There are some things that cause us great pain, but we make that pain our focus and not focus on where we want to go or achieve. This is also a personal choice. Our emotions keep us in a relationship with what needs to be left behind. You can be so consumed by what you want to focus on that's a picture of the pain; you can easily miss the fact that you have a flight booked to something new or somewhere new.

Step 1

In the following exercise, identify 1 to 3 of these items associated to each brick. What needs to change?

The Brick   **Identify the What and Who...**

Brick   Grow Up?   _____

_____   Change Surrounding ?   _____

                                                       Change a Relationship?   _____

Brick   Grow Up?   _____

_____   Change Surrounding ?   _____

                                                       Change a Relationship?   _____

Brick   Grow Up?   _____

_____   Change Surrounding ?   _____

                                                       Change a Relationship?   _____

Brick   Grow Up?   _____

_____   Change Surrounding ?   _____

                                                       Change a Relationship?   _____

Brick   Grow Up?   _____

_____   Change Surrounding ?   _____

                                                       Change a Relationship?   _____

Brick   Grow Up?   _____

_____   Change Surrounding ?   _____

                                                       Change a Relationship?   _____

Step 2

Create an action plan for each item as needed. Copy this page. Create a precise plan for each change you have to make and decide to act! Do not list the bricks here, just the actions you are taking.

Grow Up

_____
_____
_____

Change Surrounding

_____
_____
_____

Change a Relationship

_____
_____
_____

Grow Up

_____
_____
_____

Change Surrounding

_____
_____
_____

Change a Relationship

_____
_____
_____

Remember, not making these changes will cause you to be consumed by what you don't need in the first place. Leave it behind. Now let's journal your trip.

Notes:

Determining Your Purpose & Getting Started

Purpose has to be the anchor of your mentality. This is why it is important to own your own light, imagine your own ideas, and determine your own destiny. Having a purpose helps with dysfunction and disease. As a matter of fact, anything, outside of the idea of you being intricately associated with your own purpose, is the bedrock of disease. Your body responds to your ideas. Your body also responds to your choices. When a choice is made towards your benefit and contributes towards your destiny, your body creates better health.

Consistency towards purpose is vital. What you actually want to do is to begin to set patterns that are healthy, not concerning diet or exercise, but concerning the choices about your future that lead to greater experiences. With this, there is always a beginning point of a pattern, a starting point to a pattern, and there's an initiating energy point to every pattern. You want this initiating energy point that leads to patterns to be your purpose and not other things that can lead to distractions.

Purpose is always a choice, and you must begin to create the right foundation to make a great choice towards your purpose. Remember, extending from every purpose will be a pattern. These patterns will begin to replace old extraneous patterns that are not needed in your life. This is why it is very important to make sure that there is a purpose established in your life that becomes the ruler of your day. Ruler: both in the sense of what commands your day, and in the sense of taking some type of measurement during the course of your day, so you can make sure that you're staying on track.

Owning your purpose, or better stated, owning your own light, is the initiating point to the patterns you want in your life. It all starts with you. It must start with you. Any other starting points will lead to unsatisfactory ends. That is a guarantee.

Step 1

Name Your Passion

_____
_____
_____
_____

What is your pain? Pain is what is registered as an experience when you feel the distance from where you are and where you want to be.

What is the point of passion at the end of your pain?

_____
_____
_____
_____

This pain actually stems from the associations that are related to where you really want to go. As a result the qualities of the people around you have become you.

Now you have to be ruthlessly honest with yourself.

What are your weaker qualities that are associated with people who were not your mentor, the people who are not doing what you're doing, and those don't support you?

1. _____
2. _____
3. _____
4. _____
5. _____
6. _____
7. _____
8. _____
9. _____
10. _____

You must be aware that your weaker qualities tie you to your pain and keeps you in the place of pain. Let me be absolutely firm in this next comment. More the 85% of all physical ailments, bodily pain, and diseases stem from the pain of not living your purpose and passion. Your pain makes points. You must be mindful of your connections.

Your quality of life stems from the quality of the people you associate with. You can be an eagle surrounded by chickens and waste your ability to fly and soar. Take inventory. Out of the weaker chicken qualities you have stated, what of the people you involve yourself with has any one of these particular qualities? Believe me, they are there. Again, be painfully honest with yourself. If you're not where you want to be, it's time to make these changes and create the lines of intelligence that will cause you to soar.

Step 2

Refocus on the three types of persons needing a life to establish your purpose; mentor, like-minded, supportive.

Notice the eagle qualities of these people. You can tell the eagles by their results. Never hope for a person to be an eagle then list them based on your hope.

1. **Take your address book or your contact list in your phone. Put in or leave in the eagles and delete the chickens.**
2. **Schedule calls and have short conversations with the three types of affected persons.**
3. **At some point facilitate activities whether they are causal or even business with the people who show up in your three types of affected persons.**
4. **Create cycles with them; facilitate periodic events and connection times.**

This creates an environment for purpose. Notice how things flow with these people. Now grow this environment. Make these types of connections a habit.

If you say, I can't find these types of people; you must recognize the issue is never an issue of finding these people. It's an issue of letting go of the people you don't need. You cannot board the airplane to your new life carrying items that will keep you off the flight. When you finally let go of these items and board the plane, guess what? Everybody on the flight is headed to the same destination that you are headed to.

Step 3

Let go of the chickens. Let go of the items that keep you from moving forward. Start with something easy. Make a list of items in your house or office that has not served you in any way in the past year.

1. _____
2. _____
3. _____
4. _____
5. _____
6. _____
7. _____
8. _____
9. _____
10. _____

Call the Salvation Army or Goodwill Industries and schedule a pick up.

 Seeing, Calling, Interacting, Conversing, Spending Time with, and Giving to...

1. _____
2. _____
3. _____
4. _____
5. _____
6. _____
7. _____
8. _____
9. _____
10. _____

In order to start some things, there will always be other things you will have to stop. Energy is very unforgiving and accurate. You cannot dial into one frequency and hope and pray for an all together different result. Once you create an energy vortex, all the knowledge needed is contained in that vortex of relationships. Let's use flying on an airline as an example.

Step 4

Now with this new sense of clarity, state your purpose for life.

_____
_____
_____

List a few specific goals associated with your purpose.

1. _____
2. _____
3. _____
4. _____
5. _____

How do you get what you want in life? It all starts with your ability to plant what you want in life inside your body, so that one day it can exist outside your body. This is your primary role in the success of your own greatness. We would discuss this in detail in the next chapter, but you must know the value of your relationships. Your relationships contribute to one of the largest parts of your internal compositional make-ups, invested in the establishment of your greatness. This is a major key of fulfillment. Who you surround yourself with determines the mirror image of your end results. So you must,

1. Plant the seed of your purpose
2. Surround yourself with the right relationships
3. Your body will then time out your success

It is the first two that prepare you for your greatness and your destiny. You determine your own light, then you building the right relationships around your idea, and the light that goes off in your head. In order to do this, you must establish the intelligence of your dream. When you set your purpose, that purpose not only carries a live energy like a frequency, but it also carries an intelligence within that energy. You must consciously raise the intelligence of your focus and your mindset to match the intelligence of what you want to accomplish.

Determining Your Approach

Higher accomplishments carry higher levels of intelligence. This is natural. Meaning, you cannot approach great accomplishments with low intelligence. So I will teach you a system of intelligence that will help you to gain a better understanding of where you are in your intelligence with respect to where you want to be in your purpose. I will introduce you to the Intelligence Stratum.

The Intelligence Stratum contains eight levels of intelligence that range from primal intelligence to an all-knowing intelligence. I will describe each one individually, but every individual spans in the entire range of the intelligence stratum. Most, of the human population, reside between the basic intelligence and the coordinal intelligence, but there are quite a few people that are predominately primal in nature. As you go through the definitions, you will begin to understand where the people, who are around you, reside. Most importantly, you must understand and know the level of intelligence on which you reside. This covers the following:

1. How you approach your dream.
2. Your level of awareness of what you want, and your purpose.
3. Your decision-making ability.
4. Your outlook on life.

Here are the levels of intelligence in the Intelligence Stratum:

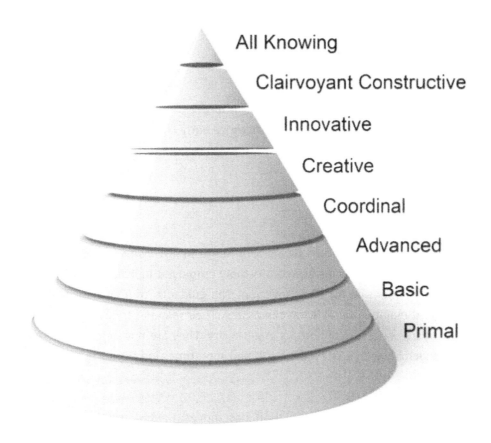

I will give a short description and characteristics of each component starting with the primal. As I describe these, keep in mind that each level of human existence is characterized by

1. How one views the world.
2. How one responds to what's in front of him or her.
3. How one is governed.
4. How one approaches, actionably, what they want in life.

Primal

The primal person is characterized by a survival mentality. There is no real sense of government or a thin relationship to governing entities. Consequently, primal humans are governed by the environment. These are people who primarily live from day to day with no real plan of action. They usually respond to situations without surety, and with fear or frustration. You can, usually, pick these characteristics up in their behavior patterns and language. Holding a job is sporadic, if a job is an option at all. Primal people use superficial bolstering to master or control a situation due to the inability to ponder and think things through. Decision making can be direct and movements are primal in nature. Sex is basic, and the intensity of sexuality can be without intimacy.

You must understand that at one point, the entirety of the human population was at this state of maturity and intelligence. You can also characterize early childhood from birth to about 3-4 years of age as primal.

Basic

The "basic" person is characterized by a strong sense of government and the need for a higher human order or hierarchy. These people are comfortably employed individuals who need the structure of the boss/employee relationship for basic function. The guidance of a civil society is important to them in order to live and maintain basic living conditions. They respond to situations by looking to those, who might carry the answers, or from others in authority. They are not as fearful or frustrated as the primal, but they approach life with apathy, distance, and sometimes indifference. They can take what comes.

A good number of the human population has moved passed the primal and live within the basic intelligence stratum. This can also characterize children of school age who are dependent on external structure for everyday existence.

Advanced

This is the part of the population that is considered to be more "spiritual" in nature. They are governed by God, or a deep since of belief in God or any other supreme invisible being. They are generally part of a collective and find their comfort there. They can be characterized by a sense of courage and generally carry a greater sense of hope, although it might be tied to a specific belief or religion. These people find themselves, generally, at a better rank of living and can make good managers and home makers. They respond to situations based on their faith and usually would have to wait on divine guidance when it comes to their decision making.

Human evolution has placed a great number of people in this stratum. It is also here, however, that people can lose a sense of self in sacrifice to a supreme being or their religion.

Coordinal

This stratum is characterized by people who can be extremely self-sufficient. They can be religious, but they are generally governed by what they see and the order of what they see. With respect to this stage of human maturity, existing at this stratum is the beginning of the recognition of self-power. They cannot stand for things to be out of place. They respond to situations by placing things in order and then managing that order. They have an extreme since of pride and are known for getting things done. These people can find themselves in upper management and are very dependable.

Coordinal people can handle what's in front of them. Where there is disorder, they can recognize it and place things in order for functionality.

Creative

Creative people can scare a coordinal person. They can see the same disorder and instead of placing things back in order, they can take what is seen and create a new order that still works. They are not necessarily governed by what is known, but can be governed by possibilities of the unknown. They are able to push against the unknown and creatively come up with solutions that can be satisfactory. They can be good managers, but they characterize the beginning of leadership, so they can also make great directors and entrepreneurs. They approach situations with little fear because they can be confident in their creative ability.

As far as human maturity and potential, the population rests currently between a basic and advanced level of intelligence with a few creative people peaking up in many cultures that provide leadership.

Innovative

An innovative person is similar to the creative person but with one major difference. A creative person can make things work based on what's there, whereas, an innovative person can see what's not there and work off an invisible model. Innovative people are governed by what will be. They see the future, and they live their future within their present. These are the CEOs and the extreme entrepreneurs. They approach life with a vision so solid that outside situations and distractions do not garner their attention. They are rarely tied to external events that have little or nothing to do with what they want to accomplish, and they have an innate drive towards their vision.

Every generation produces many innovative people, but as time passes, being innovative will be a more common trait among the population.

Clairvoyant Constructive

The Clairvoyant Constructive are special people. They are, much the same as, the innovative person, but with an extended quality. The clairvoyant, just like the innovative person, can see what others can't see, but with less of an effort to come up with what can't be seen. Being able to see what others can't see is more of who the clairvoyant constructive person is. What's in front of them rarely bothers them because they are already in a different place. In addition, they have more of a tendency to act on what they see beyond what is, and for that reason, you now have the meaning of being constructive. They can innovate and construct the innovation at the same time. When they see something new, they almost begin to develop the new idea immediately.

There are people throughout history that fall in this category which includes individuals such as Galileo, Leonardo Di Vinci, Sam Walton, Bill Gates and the like. What's interesting is that this is not a gift, but can be learned once one is aware that all mankind hold the same potential of all levels of intelligence.

All Knowing

Here are the rarest of rare people. "All knowing" is self-explanatory, but I can use this part to explain the entirety of the Intelligence Stratum. Every person has reached a point at times where they are so sure of what's ahead of them that they have this great sense of being undeterred. Most think that the gift of all knowing is assigned only to God or "the gods", but this is entirely untrue. Every person, within their scope of intelligence, spans the entire range of the intelligence stratum from Primal to All Knowing. The level a person lives on is based on one's awareness of what they can be. This also determines how one approaches life and make decisions. The Intelligence Stratum is also the basis of a person's outlook on life. So here again are the four areas that these 8 stratums affect:

1. One's level of awareness.
2. One's approach to life's situations.
3. How one makes decisions, or even one's capability of making decisions.
4. One's outlook.

You can approach life from the standpoint of being primal, or even approach a decision from a standpoint of being primal, and then you have some people who make their decisions from a coordinal point of view for example. Again, the stratum is to help you to strengthen your choice towards your purpose. When you find yourself making a decision from a primal point of view, by being aware of the stratum, you can purposefully move through the chart to a more effective point of view.

When it comes to your mind, you must first ask the question, where is your mind? From what position do you emanate your thought processes? How do you categorize what you think? Is it primal? Listen to the language you use. Are you fighting to get things done? Are you consistently frustrated? What are you being aware of? Are you aware of what needs to be fixed (Primal), or are you aware of what can be created (Creative), or can you sit for a moment and allow something new to come to your mind (Innovative)?

Do you need to pray about it (Advanced), or are you focused on setting things in order (Coordinal)? What you must be aware of, is that you can determine the condition of your mind by choice. It is a matter paying attention to your thinking and not taking your approach for granted. Design your approach by activating a level of intelligence that is more suited for dream building.

When it comes to "who you are" or your level of being, you can ask the same questions. Who are you in the moment? Better yet, you can determine this before you live in your moments. There are times you have to deliberately say, "Before anything happens, I am not going to be primal, but I will approach this from the standpoint of innovation!" You might be a person of faith (Advanced), but in certain situations you have to be more determined to make a decision beyond "praying" about it and then waiting for a mystery to unfold. In this case, it takes greater faith to move forward based on what you know is right (Clairvoyant Constructive).

Think of the Intelligence Stratum as a thermometer.

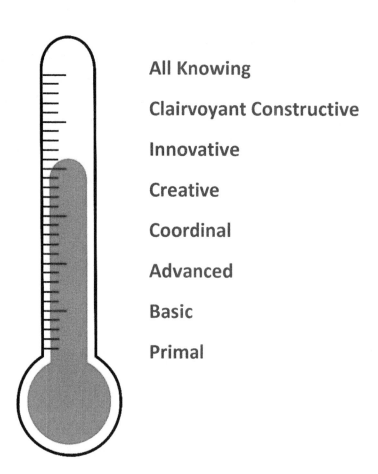

All Knowing

Clairvoyant Constructive

Innovative

Creative

Coordinal

Advanced

Basic

Primal

What you want to do here is raise the temperature of your awareness, your approach, your ability to make decisions, and your outlook. It concerns how you think, who you are, how you feel, and then how you present yourself to the world as you remember what to be. Your future choices are memory channels that can and will offset unwanted memories.

What you want to be able to do is to change the temperature, of your outlook and approach, at any given time. Your purpose depends on how you make your choices because your level of intelligence is what makes you capable of superior focus, by keeping your thoughts on your where you are going. It opens the window by allowing you to know who you are in a world that is shifting in nature. Meaning, when things around you change, you don't change. It contributes to how you feel by helping maintain balanced emotions. For example, you have a determined purpose and you are working on that light, and then something unexpected happens:

1. The primal person gets upset and says forget it.
2. The basic person says I can't do this without help.
3. An advanced person will seek God's guidance.
4. A coordinal person will organize the situation and bring it under control.
5. A creative person will reorganize the situation and do something new.
6. An innovative person will see something new and then act.
7. A clairvoyant constructive person will make something new based on what they see.
8. An all knowing knows what to do beyond fear.

You must memorize this system! It is vital to where you are in your actions and approach. If you are not quite getting the results you want, you must take inventory of how you are thinking and then your behavior patterns. You must ask, "Am I thinking primal? Am I behaving primal?" If so, you must raise the temperature of your intelligence. The higher the temperature of your intelligence, the quicker you can access your results. I suggest you at least start your approach for everything at a creative level, and then try to move up from there.

1. When restating your past bricks into new statements following a strong proclamation of "I am enough", try being creative in your new statements. Get rid of primal and basic thoughts.

2. When you are settings the three types of effective people in your life, be creative, be innovative. Staying primal will keep primal people circling around you like sharks. Remember, this applies to obtaining a mentor, recognizing and engaging persons who are likeminded and doing what you do, and establishing supportive relationships.

3. When determining your purpose, move your level of thinking to innovative. Relax and let information come to you being opening up to the aspects of your clairvoyant self. You know the answers. This involves letting go of lower levels of intelligence. Again, it's about getting out of your own way.

This exercise is simple, but it takes absolute honesty with yourself.

1. Write down your current approach to each of these 3.
2. Then check the temperature level of that approach.
3. Cross out the lower level, check a higher level creative and above.
4. Rewrite a new thought statement and action statement associated with the higher level.

1. List your current approach in writing your new responses: _____

_____
_____
_____

All Knowing _____

Clairvoyant Constructive _____

Innovative _____

Creative _____

Coordinal _____

Advanced _____

Basic _____

Primal _____

Cross out the old check and write in your new level of intelligence: _____

Write in your new language using the energy of the intelligence level you desire.

_____
_____
_____
_____

2. List your current approach in setting 3 effective relationships: _____

_____
_____
_____

All Knowing _____

Clairvoyant Constructive _____

Innovative _____

Creative _____

Coordinal _____

Advanced _____

Basic _____

Primal _____

Cross out the old check and write in your new level of intelligence: _____

Write in your new language using the energy of the intelligence level you desire.

_____
_____
_____
_____

3. List your current approach in determining your purpose: _____

_____
_____
_____

All Knowing _____

Clairvoyant Constructive _____

Innovative _____

Creative _____

Coordinal _____

Advanced _____

Basic _____

Primal _____

Cross out the old check and write in your new level of intelligence: _____

Write in your new language using the energy of the intelligence level you desire.

_____
_____
_____
_____

Creating Great Relationships

What you want to do is create the energy of progression around the following components of who you are.

1. Heart
2. Soul
3. Mind
4. Body

The energy of your relationship are contained in the following:

The 8 Ordinances of Relationships & The 12 Points of Significance

1. Presence
2. Potential
3. Progress
4. Pace
5. Promise
6. Participation
7. Promotion
8. Provision

1. To be Viewed
2. To be Understood
3. To be Engaged
4. To be Praised
5. To be Believed
6. To be Prioritized
7. To be Enriched
8. To be Advanced
9. To be Rewarded
10. To be Exalted
11. To be Increased
12. To be Mirrored

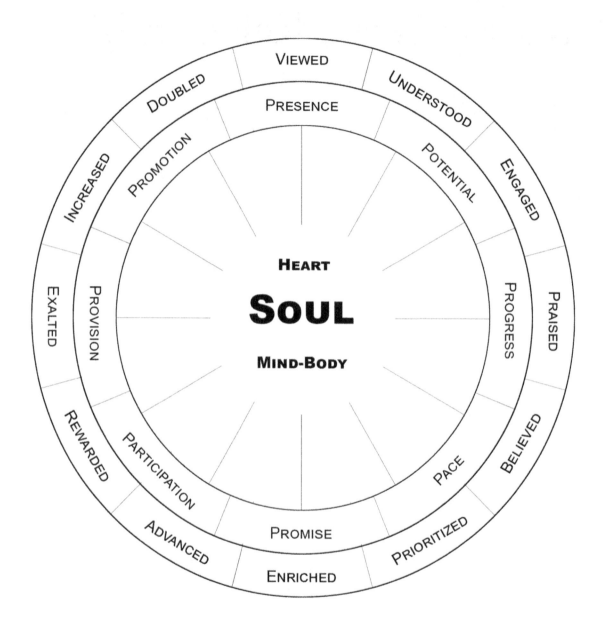

The outer circle represents the 12 Points of Significance. These are 12 points by which you can measure your relationships and assess when, where, and how people are involved with you. I call them investments that supply you with significance. This significance becomes an energy that can and will propel you towards your dream.

You must remember that everything is energy and energy has two components. People are the first part of your extended existence that you would want to measure and should be consistent with who you are. This becomes the balancing part of your energy at its source. Your economy starts with your relationship with others and their relationship towards you. It feels good when people can respond to your needs. It is even better when people see your needs and respond to you without you even having to ask. It is even greater when people can be so tuned into who you are that they meet your need before it even becomes a need. This not only gives you significance, but because energy is not spent here, you are immediately enabled to see "the more" in your life and move to your next levels due to people having your back.

Here are 12 points of significance that should be measures and engaged or you can see these as the 12 energy dynamics to a great relationship:

1

(To Be Viewed)

The Investment of seeing and knowing a person.

- To know a person as in their habits, favorite things, concerns etc.

- To be concerned and having a person's back based on what you see in them.

- See, recognize, and care for one's issues.

Everyone needs someone to see and know who they are.

2

(To Be Comprehended)

The Investment of understanding a person.

- Understanding of one's issues.

- Willing to take in right information concerning a person.

- Agreement and right action towards that understanding of the person.

Everyone has a need to be understood.

3

(To Be Engaged)

The Investment of active commitment.

- Physical connection.

- Partnership and unification.

- Two way exchange or communication.

Everyone has a need to be touched in some way.

4

(To Be Praised)

The Investment of vocal affirmation of the good.

- Recognition and hearing about good attributes.

- Complimentary in nature towards a person.

- Approvals of ideas, thoughts, visions...etc.

Everyone has a need to hear something good about themselves.

5

(To Be Believed)

The Investment of trust.

- Take a position based on concerns verbalized, or character exuded.

- Action oriented belief qualified by action oriented support.

- Taking responsibility and acting on a person's behalf based believing in them.

Everyone has a need to be trusted and believed in.

6

(To Be Prioritized)

The Investment of making one special.

- Acute attention in certain situations and areas.

- Putting things aside in recognition of the other.

- Allowing a person from time to time to be the most important.

Everyone has the need to feel number one sometimes.

7

(To Be Enriched)

The Investment of provision.

- Bringing gifts or supplies not associated with earning.

- Sharing your personal substance.

- Making sure a person's needs are met.

Everyone has a need to receive.

8

(To Be Advanced)

The Investment of pushing one forward.

- Progressing one's effort by means of time and efforts.

- Providing leadership in your area of expertise to advance the cause of another.

- To give an effort in setting a situation or circumstance right.

Everyone has a need to be mentored or pushed forward.

9

(To Be Rewarded)

The Investment of recognition.

- To provide substance in recognition of what someone has invested in you.

- Physical substance given in appreciation for efforts made.

- Thank you and appreciation outside of verbal affirmation.

Everyone has a need to be appreciated in a tangible way.

10

(To Be Exalted)

The Investment of one's self into another.

- Time spent in all areas of emotional investments.

- Giving a sense of place based on your presence.

- The gift of yourself that lift a person to another level, give status or empowers.

Everyone has a need to feel another's presence that builds their own presence.

11

(To Be Increased)

The Investment of addition.

- To empower, enhance or enable in any way.

- To see then add in a positive way time, effort, or substance.

- To be an extension for someone where someone comes short.

Everyone has a need to be completed by the investment of another's effort and partnership.

12

(To Be Doubled)

The Investment of multiplication.

- The experience of results.

- Results that lead to more results.

- Results that give a sense of place, home, completeness.

Everyone has a need to grow by the investment of another's effort or partnership.

As you can see... your relationships and how they are set, play a vital role in your ability to see and experience your life at its best. This is the true beginning of everything economic. Remember, energy is personal psychological money. In order to live a fuller and more exiting life, you must prepare yourself to receive your full supply of what's for you by setting your perception and aligning your relationships in order to keep focused on your own good and producing good.

Step 1

Start documenting the persons who fit into these 12 slots. Remember your words and language is important to your personal development. With this being the case, you want to enable yourself to have quality conversations. These 12 types of relative energy dynamics will provide the basis for empowering conversations.

1

(To Be Viewed)

Who sees who you are and respects that?

The Investment of seeing and knowing a person.

_____
_____
_____
_____
_____
_____
_____
_____

Everyone needs someone to see and know who they are.

2

(To Be Comprehended)

Who understands you? Who understands your ideas and language?

The Investment of understanding a person.

_____
_____
_____
_____
_____
_____
_____
_____

Everyone has a need to be understood.

3

(To Be Engaged)

Who gets actively involved in what you are doing?

The Investment of active commitment.

_____
_____
_____
_____
_____
_____
_____
_____

Everyone has a need to be touched in some way.

4

(To Be Praised)

Who pays you kind words? Who are the people who can see and say the good?

The Investment of vocal affirmation of the good.

_____
_____
_____
_____
_____
_____
_____
_____

Everyone has a need to hear something good about themselves.

5

(To Be Believed)

Who trusts you because of you? Who rapidly responds to you based on trust?
The Investment of trust.

_____

_____

_____

_____

_____

_____

_____

_____

Everyone has a need to be trusted and believed in.

6

(To Be Prioritized)

Who takes the time from time to time to put you first?
The Investment of making one special.

_____

_____

_____

_____

_____

_____

_____

Everyone has the need to feel number one sometimes.

7

(To Be Enriched)

Who gives to you just because?

The Investment of provision.

_____
_____
_____
_____
_____
_____
_____
_____

Everyone has a need to receive.

8

(To Be Advanced)

Who pushes you to the next level?

The Investment of pushing one forward.

_____
_____
_____
_____
_____
_____
_____
_____

Everyone has a need to be mentored or pushed forward.

9

(To Be Rewarded)

Who sees your contributions and acts towards it through recognizing you in a tangible way?
The Investment of recognition.

_____

_____

_____

_____

_____

_____

_____

_____

Everyone has a need to be appreciated in a tangible way.

10

(To Be Exalted)

Who gives you their support, but not just in words or verbal sentiment? Who shows up?
The Investment of one's self into another.

_____

_____

_____

_____

_____

_____

_____

_____

Everyone has a need to feel another's presence that builds their own presence.

11

(To Be Increased)

Who gives you their time and talent in areas that you are not the best in?

The Investment of addition.

_____
_____
_____
_____
_____
_____
_____
_____

Everyone has a need to be completed by the investment of another's effort and partnership.

12

(To Be Doubled)

Who agrees with you and is willing to act towards that agreement?

The Investment of multiplication.

_____
_____
_____
_____
_____
_____
_____
_____

Everyone has a need to grow by the investment of another's effort or partnership.

Step 2

Make sure you enact these same points of significance towards others.

1

(View Someone)

The Investment of seeing and knowing a person.

Everyone needs someone to see and know who they are.

2

(Comprehended Someone)

The Investment of understanding a person.

Everyone has a need to be understood.

3

(Engage Someone)

The Investment of active commitment.

Everyone has a need to be touched in some way.

4

(Give Someone Praise)

The Investment of vocal affirmation of the good.

Everyone has a need to hear something good about themselves.

5

(Believe in Someone)

The Investment of trust.

Everyone has a need to be trusted and believed in.

6

(Prioritize Someone)

The Investment of making one special.

Everyone has the need to feel number one sometimes.

7

(Enrich Someone's Life)

The Investment of provision.

Everyone has a need to receive.

8

(Advance Someone)

The Investment of pushing one forward.

Everyone has a need to be mentored or pushed forward.

9

(Reward Someone)

The Investment of recognition.

Everyone has a need to be appreciated in a tangible way.

10

(Exalt Someone)

The Investment of one's self into another.

Everyone has a need to feel another's presence that builds their own presence.

11

(Increase Someone)

The Investment of addition.

Everyone has a need to be completed by the investment of another's effort and partnership.

12

(Be Someone's Double)

The Investment of multiplication.

Everyone has a need to grow by the investment of another's effort or partnership.

This gives the totality of your energy its balance. That's why it is vital to document and measure these 12 points. Relationships become a vital part of self-recognition. It is within the self that all knowledge is contained. Without the right people around you, it becomes difficult to draw on this knowledge. Many people spend thousands of dollars to institutions and individuals seeking higher knowledge, but all knowledge is contained within. You can serve as your own model.

The 8 Ordinances of Relationships

You want to make sure that there is a balance between the heart, the soul, and the mind-body dynamic. I would like to provide you with a guideline to assist you with this called the 8 Ordinances of Relationship. I will give you a short definition of each and then you can add them into the 12 Points of Significance. The combination of these guidelines will give you a clear picture of how you order the relationships around you. Here's the second list. You should inspect each of these within the three categories of friendship, personal relationships, and mentorship.

1. Presence
2. Potential
3. Pace
4. Progress
5. Promise
6. Participation
7. Provision
8. Promotion

Here are the definitions.

1. Presence

Within the context of all of your relationships a person should provide you with presence. Their presence or their mere presence should contribute to the energy of who you are. You should have an extreme sense of comfort in the presence of this person.

2. Potential

Every relationship you're in should carry potential. You should be able to immediately ascertain where a relationship is going and what the results of the relationship should be. Every new relationship starts with a blank slate, but importance should be placed as to determining what's going to fill that slate as the relationship progresses.

3. Pace

Every relationship should have a set pace. There should be expectation at all times of some type of completion. And then the expectation should be set in order and practiced. Every relationship should be going somewhere.

4. Progress

Over the course of time, you should be measuring progress. This is an essential part of your relationship. There should always be growth in a relationship. And there should always be growth towards something in which two or more of you are working on together.

5. Promise

Integrity should be a part of a relationship. There have to be commitments made towards the goal of each person within the relationship. Those commitments should be prioritized and completed. This has to be a definite expectation.

6. Participation

There must be conscious active participation with respect to the goals of the individuals involved in a relationship. There must be keen awareness of what the person is doing and then a commitment of viable activity towards it.

7. Provision

In every relationship you should expect some provision. If a person is focused on what you're doing there should be some type of provision, whether it is an investment of time, an investment of money, or the investment of expertise.

8. Promotion

In addition to just measuring progress, you should also be measuring linear progression and promotion. Promotion is exponential growth. You should expect this within the context of your relationship at different time periods as it relates to pace to be at higher levels. Promotion also involves each spreading and sharing the efforts of the other to increase each other's profiting, progression, and prosperity.

Exercise

Take measurement of the type people you have in your life. Determine what they offer in each category. As you make your lists, also make planes to engage the people on the right more.

1. Presence

Who doesn't have presence?

_____
_____
_____
_____
_____

Who has presence?

_____
_____
_____
_____
_____

2. Potential

Who doesn't have potential?

_____
_____
_____
_____
_____

Who has potential?

_____
_____
_____
_____
_____

3. Pace

Who doesn't keeps up with you?

_____
_____
_____
_____
_____

Who keeps up with you?

_____
_____
_____
_____
_____

4. Progress

Who doesn't help your progress?

_____
_____
_____
_____
_____

Who helps you to progress?

_____
_____
_____
_____
_____

5. Promise

Who doesn't keep their word?

_____

_____

_____

_____

_____

Who keeps their word?

_____

_____

_____

_____

_____

6. Participation

Who doesn't participate in your dream?

_____

_____

_____

_____

_____

Who participates in your dream?

_____

_____

_____

_____

_____

7. Provision

Who doesn't invest in you?

_____

_____

_____

_____

_____

Who invests in you?

_____

_____

_____

_____

_____

8. Promotion

Who doesn't promote you?   Who promotes you?

_____   _____

_____   _____

_____   _____

_____   _____

_____   _____

With each level of relationship or each type of relationship, the 8 Ordinances of Relationship is a guideline that works for all. Remember, these three levels of relationship should open you up to your own light and ideas. If you're feeling closed in and stuck, it is because of the relationships you currently have. You need to become comfortable with making the necessary arrangements to deal with better people or more progressive persons. Remember that your heart, your soul, and your mind-body dynamic are impacted by behavior patterns that are focused on you. In turn, you are provided with the energy to do great things. With this you must monitor, manage, and master all of your relationships, which also protects your idea.

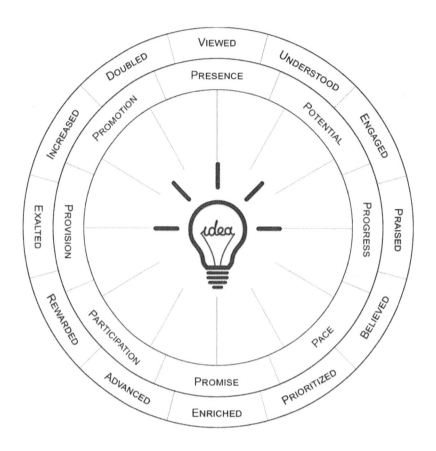

Your Approach to Your Relationships

Complete the same exercise when it comes to your relationships. What's your level of intelligence when it comes to determining who you're interacting with? _____

You can copy this page and use it for your relationships overall or go through each relationship point one by one.

All Knowing   _____

Clairvoyant Constructive   _____

Innovative   _____

Creative   _____

Coordinal   _____

Advanced   _____

Basic   _____

Primal   _____

Cross out the old check and write in your new level of intelligence: _____

Write in your new language using the energy of the intelligence level you desire.

_____

_____

_____

_____

Strategies for Growth

Growth moves from the stage of physical growing to the stage of economical types of growth that continue outside of the body. Both sides are driven by the same hormones.

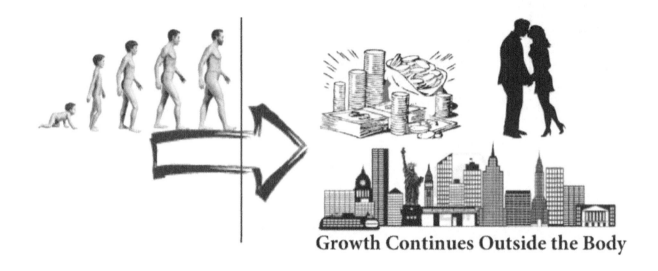

Growth Continues Outside the Body

Mankind is the only entity that can develop an existence outside of himself that mirrors his ambition, and there be no limits placed on that existence, in terms of growth. Everyone has dreams, but not everyone is capable of living their dreams because they don't understand the fundamentals of growth. Purpose has to be at the root of your psychological existence.

Simply put, whatever you think about the most is who you are. This is why it is so important that you choose a purpose. If your thoughts are directed towards outside entities, circumstances, issues, and movements, it becomes who you are. This is the law of the universe. Everything grows. So really, we're not even dealing with an issue of growing, but an issue of focus. Purpose is equivalent to a seed. Both require focus.

Purpose is always in a state of growth. So we're not dealing with whether or not you can grow your dream, we are dealing with your ability to grow into your dream. If your dream is not growing, you can rest assured that something else, whether it be something that you like or not, is growing instead. When a seed is planted, it will be what it is. There is no question about that. Your human mind-body and soul system works in this exact manner by design. You just have to determine your seed or purpose. Get started. When this is done you set the stage for exponential growth.

Exercise

- Identify what you would like to accomplish and break it down into 4, 8 or 12 part units. Each one of these units will represent a chamber of time. Make sure you have a succession of relationships set stemming from the 12 points of significance.

- You must energize each one of these units or time chamber by executing profitable relationships by the process of authentication. This will help with setting your frequency to these time chambers.

    - You build each time chamber by organizing and starting your project.
    - You then energize the time chamber setting expectations of your results, and by requiring the energy of investment from those you are engaged and associated with.
    - Authenticate your effort by engaging your mentor for direction and help, then remaining consistent in your actions on a daily basis towards your project.
    - Complete your first time chamber which opens you up to what to do in the next time chamber.

- Now you can set each chamber in time to achieve your results. To do this, you must push time in front of a natural cycle or season. This means that you do what's optimal in each time chamber. It's just like planting a seed; you have to plant it within the right cycle. The same works when a child is conceived, you see the results brought about by time.

Samples of the time chambers. I will show you how to set them up and fill them in.

	Viewed	Comprehended		Engaged	
Enriched					Praised
Advanced	Build	Build	Build	Build	Believed
Rewarded	Energize	Energize	Energize	Energize	Prioritized
	Authenticate	Authenticate	Authenticate	Authenticate	
	Complete	Complete	Complete	Complete	
	Exalted	Doubled		Increased	

	Viewed	Comprehended		Engaged	
Enriched					Praised
Advanced					Believed
Rewarded					Prioritized
	Exalted	Doubled		Increased	

	Viewed	Comprehended		Engaged	
Enriched					Praised
Advanced					Believed
Rewarded					Prioritized
	Exalted	Doubled		Increased	

1.   Set Your Project

When setting your project into 4, 8 or 12 chambers, you are not setting them into to 4-12 equal parts, but 4-12 exponential parts. This is important because you are setting the stage for growth. You will use the accomplishment of the first chamber to create the basis for accomplishing the next. Work within one chamber at a time. Complete your first chamber first. Completing your first chamber sets the energy for all other chambers.

Project A

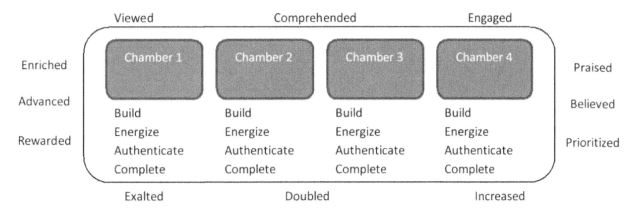

Start   **Finish**

Again for each chamber you have to set forth these four practices:

1. Build
2. Energize
3. Authenticate
4. Complete

Then you move to the next chamber.

2.   Set Your Relationships

You are also surrounding what you do with 12 points of significance. List below a person or persons that will deliver you a point of significance. A single individual can cover multiple points. Be sure to read the details of these points in the appendix, and make sure that the individuals are consistent with each point of significance.

Point	Person 1	Person 2	Person 3
Who Views You			
Who Comprehends You			
Who Engages You			
Who Praises You			
Who Believes in You			
Who Prioritizes You			
Who Enriches You			
Who Advances You			
Who Rewards You			
Who Exalts You			
Who Increases You			
Who Doubles You			

3.   Infuse Previous Experience

Here, you will take advantage of the past experiences of your own and the past experience of others to advance your projects. Engage your mentors. List the books, classes, seminars, names of mentors and advisors needed to give your project a foundation and that will also speed up your processes. Be sure to focus on what you have decided as your purpose, as you will need to have those at the forefront of your consciousness as you complete your task. Choose the appropriate books, classes, seminars, mentors, advisors. Also list 3 past accomplishments of your own as this contributes to your motivation.

Points of Focus	1	2	3
Books			
Classes & Courses			
Seminars			
Mentors			
Advisors			
Past Accomplishments			

4.   Set Your Timing

Use the charts below to determine what the goal of each chamber will be. Determine the overall goal of project A. For the most part, use whatever numerical value that is descriptive of your goal as your base number or your top cycle number – we will use a top sales goal in this example. Then use the charts below to help with your breakdown. Start with your top cycle number then multiply your top cycle number by the respective percentage to get a point of accomplishment for each time chamber.

C1	C2	C3	C4
24%	38%	62%	100%

C1	C2	C3	C4	C5	C6	C7	C8
4%	6%	9%	15%	24%	38%	62%	100%

C1	C2	C3	C4	C5	C6	C7	C8	C9	C10	C11	C12
.3%	.5%	1%	2%	4%	6%	9%	15%	24%	38%	62%	100%

Here's a sample if you used the chart for 4 chambers with the top cycle being 1000 sales. There are many types of accomplishments; I am using sales in this example of sales because it covers a broader base of applications, but I will list other examples shortly.

Here when you set your task into 4 chambers, you have 4 cycles to complete. If your final effort is 100 sales, then you use the 4 chamber chart, in which your first chamber is 24% of your top cycle.

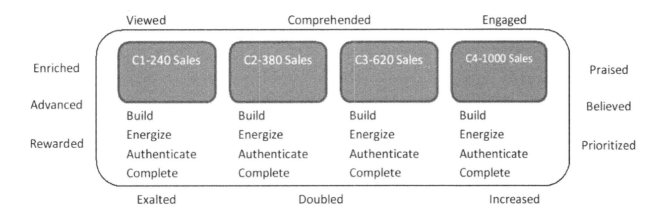

Here's a sample if you used the chart for 12 chambers with the top cycle being 1000 sales. Using the 12 chamber chart your first chamber 3% of your top cycle goal of 1000 which is 3 sales. In this case, you never think about achieving 1000 sales, only 3 sales.

Notice I refer to each chamber as a cycle. When you set your tasks into 12 chambers, you have 12 cycles, where your first cycle is 3 sales or the equivalent in effort, and your last cycle is 1000 sales or the equivalent in effort for whatever factor is associated with what you want to accomplish. If there are no numbers associated with your task, be sure to break everything down in approximate value to the percentages given, always starting with a manageable and accomplishable first cycle or chamber 1.

These are sample charts wherein you can insert your cycle values. This strategy for growth is not just for business, but can be used for sales, behavior modification, building and growing relationships, diet plans, and some health goals. Here are a few examples.

Example 1 – Sales

If you goal is to open a bakery, but you don't have the financing or the ability to obtain financing. Plug into the last chamber what you picture yourself doing at your top cycle. Then ask yourself, "What can I afford to bake now?" If it's only 3 pies, put that in your first chamber cycle to bake 3 pies. In your second chamber cycle put in for example, 3 pies and 2 cakes and so on...Start. Completing your first chamber will make you just as successful as completing your last.

Example 2 – Behavior Modification

Let's say you want to stop smoking. Of course you will have zero cigarettes as your last cycle. So here you cut down smoking incrementally within each cycle. Start in your first chamber with a number down from what you are currently smoking. Make sure it's a reduction that you can handle. Here you would need to take full advantage of your 12 points of significance and your authentication processes, especially adding into the mix a Major Authenticator, someone that will help you and can serve as a model.

Example 3 – Building Relationships

Since relationships are about action towards persons, you have to take measurement of your actions given and measurement of the actions presented towards you. You put into your top cycle the desired goal for the relationship or relationships, both the number and/or type. Then you determine your actions in your first chamber cycle that are congruent with what you want to accomplish and build the time chambers incrementally.

Example 4 – Health

If you are losing weight, you can work the system like the sales model when it comes to setting up the cycles. If you are setting up an exercise regimen, set within the cycles your number of reps when comes to lifting weights, doing sit-ups or any other type of exercise regimen. Here again, use your authentications to propel you through your chambers.

In all of these, you set the first cycle, accomplish the first cycle, and then use it as a base to exponentially grow all other cycles. To do this, you repeat the first cycle by creating more energy and multiplying your efforts in the second cycle. This process ties you into natural cycles and seasons that have been in existence since the beginning of time and is also imbedded in both your chemical and biological systems.

Copy the next page and apply the time chambers, cycles, and numbers to your tasks. Here the chamber key and a template to fill in the numbers.

1. Choose your final goal: financial number, physical number, ideal number ect.
2. Multiply your top number by each percentage in the selected keys: 4, 8, or 12
3. You can also use decimals if you don't have a calculator 24% is .24 / 4% is .04 / .3% is .003 etc.
4. After determining the value of each time chamber, build, energize, authenticate and complete.

C1	C2	C3	C4
24%	38%	62%	100%

C1	C2	C3	C4	C5	C6	C7	C8
4%	6%	9%	15%	24%	38%	62%	100%

C1	C2	C3	C4	C5	C6	C7	C8	C9	C10	C11	C12
.3%	.5%	1%	2%	4%	6%	9%	15%	24%	38%	62%	100%

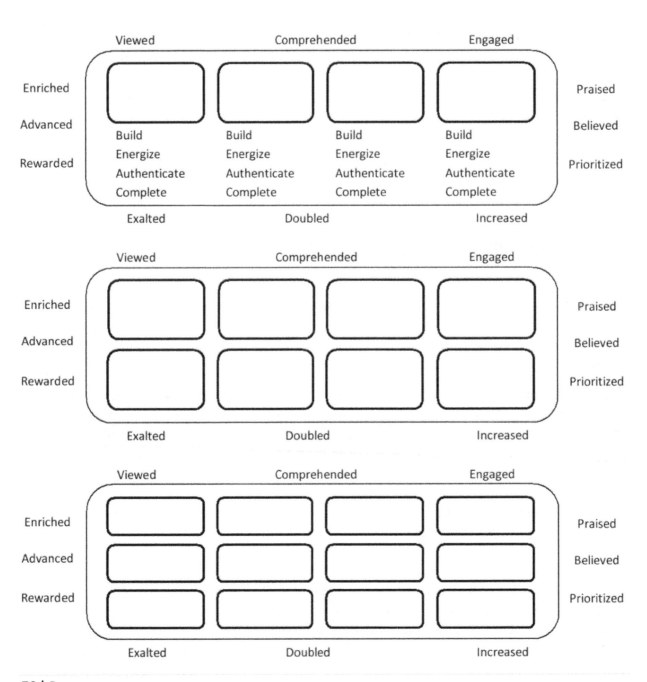

Your Approach to Growth and Growing

Complete the same exercise when it comes to your growth. What's your level of intelligence when it comes to determining your start and end points? _____

You can copy this page and use it for your growth strategies. Apply it when setting your finishing points and subsequently your starting points.

All Knowing	_____
Clairvoyant Constructive	_____
Innovative	_____
Creative	_____
Coordinal	_____
Advanced	_____
Basic	_____
Primal	_____

Cross out the old check and write in your new level of intelligence: _____

Write in your new language using the energy of the intelligence level you desire.

_____
_____
_____
_____

Build in Your Completions

To know your completions is to obtain the end results that are built into your body. It is your body; yes, your physical body that is the energy source for the idea or purpose that you're trying to accomplish. You have to know how to take advantage of the neurotransmitters and hormones that you have, which automatically contribute to what you're trying to accomplish. It is about being so in tuned with what you want, that what you want is a natural process of living without a great expenditure of energy.

Your physical makeup is designed to provide you with these types of resources. This process is the next level of visualization. Visualization has been a strong component of personal development for many years. I want to teach you a form of visualization, which works in tandem with your biological systems that is designed to do this in the most incredible ways, naturally. This lends itself entirely to the strategy of growing.

You have full control over what you think. This is why you must also take advantage of the opportunity of knowing that you must control your environment, which influences the energy of your thinking.

To accomplish completion, whether it be within a cycle of a single time chamber or completing your overall project, you must be highly considerate of your environment as every phase of your environment contributes to your success, which includes the following components.

1. Physical Environment **(Visual Environment)**
    a. Residence
    b. Office
    c. Places you decide to go
    d. Video
2. Environment of Sound **(Audible Environment)**
    a. The music you listen to
    b. The language of the persons surrounding you
    c. Incoming information towards your destiny
3. The Environment of Your Engagements **(Kinesthetic Environment)**
    a. Mentors
    b. Associations
    c. Intimate connections

Exercise 1

This will be a quick list exercise for each type of environment in order to facilitate an environment that will continuously and consistently invest in your body energy. In essence, the environment plays a major role in the maturity of your thought processes. If you're constantly thinking about a dysfunction that may be in your presence, your brain will produce a mired of neurons that will agree with that dysfunction. Once the neurotransmitters start to fire, the hormones in your body will respond in like manner. Then, physiologically, you will become more of the dysfunction that you think about.

When I speak of dysfunction, I am not necessarily speaking of anything that can be considered bad. Anything, good or bad, that is not in line with the direction you are going will set in as a dysfunction. So you must set your environment to agree with the direction you are headed in order to optimize the energy of your direction. Any signals stored in the body affect the flow of hormones. If the hormones are off set, you can end up with a situation where your mind wants to do one thing and your body will pull in an all-together different direction. So this exercise is about being aware of your environment at all times.

1. What is it in your house that you can change out that can more enhance what you are trying to achieve?

    a. Start with pictures on the wall.

    _____
    _____
    _____
    _____
    _____

    List a date to remove some pictures and put up new ones.

    Date _____

Note: You can find great canvas art work that has positive statements on them at many home stores and discount stores.

b. How is the lighting in your home? Are there places that are dark or dim? Change the lighting.

Date _____

c. What color are your walls, carpet, and drapes. Pull up picture of mansions and high end homes. Recreate a smaller version of what you see in your home. Be creative. List some things that can be changed and upgraded. Plan to make the upgrades as soon as your budget allows.

_____
_____
_____
_____
_____

Date _____

d. Make some of the same changes and upgrade in your workspace.

Start with pictures on the wall. What positive novelties do you have on your desk?

_____
_____
_____
_____
_____

List a date to remove some pictures and put up new ones.

Date _____

e. Where are some of the places you go? What type of environments are they? Each environment should leave you with a feeling of advancement. Make a check list.

Place   How do you feel?

_____   _____
_____   _____
_____   _____
_____   _____
_____   _____
_____   _____
_____   _____
_____   _____
_____   _____

You must monitor the energy of the place you go. You might have to change places where you shop. You might have to drive a further distance to go to a better shopping center or a better mall. You may have to change a church that you attend, or join a more progressive social club. You might have to attend a more advanced form of entertainment venue. There are some people's home that offer a better environment than others. The point is, everything contributes to your bottom line and you must monitor places and events.

What are some place and events that are created for your advancement, such as seminars, forums, conferences, etc. Put some these venues on your schedule. Some of them even offer social components that can replace socials situations that aren't as advantageous.

_____
_____
_____
_____
_____
_____
_____
_____
_____

      d.   Create videos of your future success for Youtube, Facebook, and Twitter.
           i.   Download pictures of things you would like to accomplish from the internet.
          ii.   Find some positive music.
        iii.   Create a video storyboard
        iv.   Use an online video editor or buy one for under $99
         v.   Use an online service to put your video together or a local expert.

2.   The Environment of Sound

      a.   Take out your Iphone, Android phone, or tablet. Write the top 10 songs in your playlist.

1. _____
2. _____
3. _____
4. _____
5. _____
6. _____
7. _____
8. _____
9. _____
10. _____

What story does your playlist tell? Is it consistent with your dream? Go on I-tunes and or other music services such as Google Play. Type in topics related to your goals and direction. Review the songs that come up. If they leave you with a great sense of positivity, then downloads those and create a new playlist. Make sure the music in your life play the story of your success.

b. Now you must pay close attention the language of what you hear. To do this you have to list the first 5 points of the 12 points of significance. The language of these personages will always be set to uplift you. When there is a shift in your energy as some people are speaking around you, and that shift is negatively impacting you, you need to remove that energy of sound from your environment. Here, the type people you need to have in your environment should always keep the audible sounds of energy towards you at a premium. List those who fit these categories.

1

(To Be Viewed)

Who sees who you are and respects that?

The Investment of seeing and knowing a person.

_____
_____
_____
_____

Everyone needs someone to see and know who they are.

2

(To Be Comprehended)

Who understands you? Who understands your ideas and language?

The Investment of understanding a person.

_____
_____
_____
_____

Everyone has a need to be understood.

3

(To Be Engaged)

Who gets actively involved in what you are doing?

The Investment of active commitment.

_____
_____
_____
_____

Everyone has a need to be touched in some way.

4

(To Be Praised)

Who pays you kind words? Who are the people who can see and say the good?

The Investment of vocal affirmation of the good.

_____
_____
_____
_____

Everyone has a need to hear something good about themselves.

5

(To Be Believed)

Who trusts you because of you? Who rapidly responds to you based on trust?

The Investment of trust.

_____
_____
_____
_____

Everyone has a need to be trusted and believed in.

Be sure to list these people and engage these people. They will carry the language of your success. Anybody not listed will strain your conversation and what you hear. If you are pushing for the success of your project or dream, you cannot afford certain types of language around you.

c. Now we need to deal with the incoming information that is within your hearing. Whether you are conscious of it or not, your body is constantly learning. A great deal of information within your audible hearing is informational and instructive in nature. With this being an absolute fact, you must play a role in what channels of hearing you expose yourself to.

    i.   Increase your conversations with your mentor.
   ii.   Increase the conversations with those who are doing the same work.
  iii.   Increase your interactions with those who support you.

Add in the next 5 persons within the 12 points of significance.

6

(To Be Prioritized)
Who takes the time from time to time to put you first?
The Investment of making one special.

_____
_____
_____
_____

Everyone has the need to feel number one sometimes.

7

(To Be Enriched)

Who gives to you just because?

The Investment of provision.

_____

_____

_____

_____

Everyone has a need to receive.

8

(To Be Advanced)

Who pushes you to the next level?

The Investment of pushing one forward.

_____

_____

_____

_____

Everyone has a need to be mentored or pushed forward.

9

(To Be Rewarded)

Who sees your contributions and acts towards it through recognizing you in a tangible way?

The Investment of recognition.

_____

_____

_____

_____

Everyone has a need to be appreciated in a tangible way.

10

(To Be Exalted)

Who gives you their support, but not just in words or verbal sentiment? Who shows up?

The Investment of one's self into another.

_____

_____

_____

_____

Everyone has a need to feel another's presence that builds their own presence.

You must list these people and monitor their presence in your life. These are the types that only support your existence, but they will offer an educational value to your hearing intake.

Finally, you must position yourself to hear your own sounds. You must know that you carry within you the entirety of your dream. Now you must "hear" your dream from yourself, which is 100 time more important than hearing the inspiration of your dream from someone else. In order to do this, you must follow the above instructions on controlling the sounds around you. You inspiration stemming from yourself can be blocked when the concurrent sounds around you are not right and optimal.

3. The Environment of Your Engagements

    a. Mentor – We've discussed business mentors, but every area of your life can use a mentor. I will list the areas, you can list 3 potential mentors you can engage if they apply.

Life Value	Mentor
Parenting & Family	_____
	_____
	_____
Culinary Skills	_____
	_____
	_____
Health & Wellness	_____
	_____
	_____
Spiritual	_____
	_____
	_____
Financial Wellness	_____
	_____
	_____
Hobbies	_____
	_____
	_____
Entertainment Mentor	_____
	_____
	_____

b. In these same areas, who benefits you greatly? Some people are meant to lead you in these areas. Who can you associate with that drives these areas in your life to higher standards? Once listed, make it a point to make these your points of engagement.

Life Value	Associates
Parenting & Family	_____
	_____
	_____
Culinary Skills	_____
	_____
	_____
Health & Wellness	_____
	_____
	_____
Spiritual	_____
	_____
	_____
Financial Wellness	_____
	_____
	_____
Hobbies	_____
	_____
	_____
Entertainment Mentor	_____
	_____
	_____

c. Your intimate relationships must reflect the same type of considerations.

These environmental changes are essential to the driving of your completions. Things get done in the right environment. What is actually happening here is that you are giving your awareness of what it takes to complete a task the opportunity to come to the forefront of your consciousness and to stay at the forefront of your consciousness. What you dream is a guaranteed fact of manifestation. The only thing that blocks the success of your completions is the information and energy it takes to accomplish your thoughts. It is called Action Potential. Action Potential is a scientific law that generates within the right environments. This is why you can't take your environment for granted. Within the right environment your plans become inevitable.

The Inevitability of Your Completions

There is a series of things that take place between the start of something and the endpoint of that same thing. Again, this is called action potential. In this case, it begins with the release of the sperm from the male's body. Upon fertilizing an egg in the female, which is a form of relationship, the egg transforms into an embryo. Then from an embryo into a growing fetus. Then from a fetus into a full functioning human body. What's pushing the transformation, at each stage, is each stage reaching its potential or filling up, which automatically pushes you into the next. Every new stage is impending at the completion or filling of the previous stage. More importantly, what I want you to recognize here is that both the presences of the sperm and the fully developed human body, even though one is developed over time, both exist simultaneously. This is because the sperm carries the full potential of the human body. Although the human body is in its fullness at one point, it really existed, in its fullness, as a sperm. We are going to walk this through, step-by-step, until the idea is firmly invested into your mind and body. So let's move on to the next point.

You and your idea are the same presence on different ends of a spectrum, so the presence of you makes the presence of your idea imminent. Even though the idea is imminent, it cannot formulate into what it is without action potential.

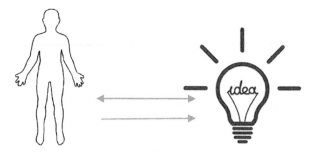

It is action potential that formulates your idea into an economic experience.

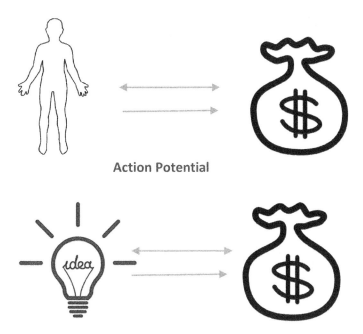

Action Potential

Your idea and the economic potential of your idea are two complete presences that exist in totality concurrently.

All of your ideas, as I stated earlier, formulate as thoughts into a physical substance in your brain called neurons, which are derived from a tiny presence called lamellipodia. The formation of these neurons happens, much in the same way, as the law of action potential.

Stage 1	Stage 2	Stage 3	Stage 4	Stage 5
Lamellipodia	Immature neurites	Axon formation	Dendrite formation	Further maturation

The lamellipodia that you see in this diagram is the beginning of a new neuron forming in your brain. This lamellipodia contains the content of your idea which makes the full-grown neuron in stage 5 imminent. The birth of this lamellipodia stems from a chain of reactions that's initiated by your thought process, and then continued by a line of water and electricity. This is the first stage of you, actually, becoming what you think. If people really knew that this is a substantial process, they would begin to guard their thought processes with all possible care and scrutiny.

This is why the seed of your thoughts cannot be planted just anywhere. In essence, the environment plays a major role in the maturity of your thought processes. If you're constantly thinking about a dysfunction that may be in your presence, your brain will produce a mired of neurons that will agree with that dysfunction. Once the neurotransmitters start to fire, the hormones in your body will respond in like manner. Then, physiologically, you will become more of the dysfunction that you think about. Via the lamellipodia, as it is extended using action potential into a fully developed neuron, your thoughts become solidified as a substance, and that substance is then mirrored as a simultaneous presence outside of yourself.

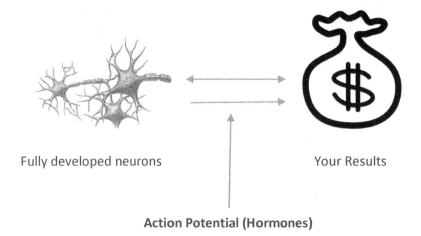

Fully developed neurons   Your Results

Action Potential (Hormones)

Stage 1	**Stage 2**	**Stage 3**	**Stage 4**	**Stage 5**
Lamellipodia	Immature neurites	Axon formation	Dendrite formation	Further maturation

The fully developed neurons that represent your thought processes are the exact same presence of who you are and what you are accomplishing. This is why what you want to accomplish is primarily a biological process. Once one end of the spectrum is in place, the other end automatically exists at the same time. Let me explain it this way. Another place where action potential is found is in the frequencies that exist between two electronic devices. Tesla, who was Thomas Edison's assistant, used the principles of action potential to promote the delivery of electricity from one point to the other. Action potential is simply how you relay a desired result from its source to another place or point.

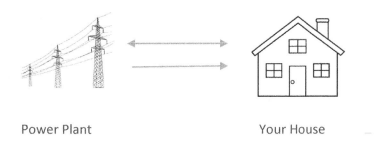

Power Plant   Your House

Action Potential (AC Current)

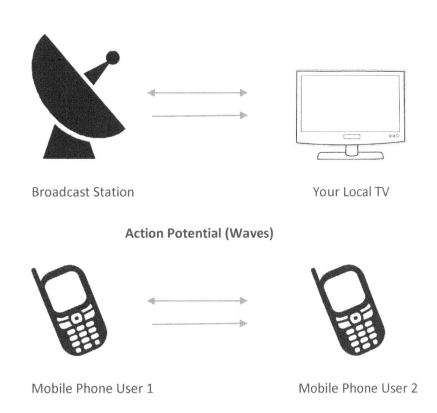

Broadcast Station   Your Local TV

Action Potential (Waves)

Mobile Phone User 1   Mobile Phone User 2

Action Potential (Frequency)

The presence of action potential causes an item that is desired and its resource to be present, concurrently. For example, the video picture that's at your local news station is the same picture on your TV. Therefore, the broadcast is located simultaneously in two different locations. When you are on a mobile phone in Chicago talking to someone in Florida, your voice is present in two different places at the same time. The same goes with how your body works. You have the source of your desire, which is the thoughts of your idea or desires. Then you have the beginning of action potential which is the neurotransmitters in your brain that affect the responding hormones. Your body goes to work right away. This is why it's so important to know your completions and to be clear about what you want, because once it is set in your body, it becomes imminent. The broadcast of your desire is set.

You might say, I visualize and think about what I want all the time, why hasn't it happened yet? It is because you haven't transferred your thought process to be reflected in your relationships and environment, and the two are firing back at you a different story and reality. Your relationships and environment also become investments into your thought processes, and if the two are not similar to what you want, they will choke out what you want. Furthermore, the activity, towards other things that are not related or similar to what you want, will burn out the energy that's needed to reach your own completions. So the thoughts of what doesn't work become prominent versus what you actually want to accomplish. If things aren't working out in your life, the "not working" just didn't happen by accident. The "not working" has its own resource and is coming from some place established within you that's now playing out its impending existence. This can happen repeatedly. What you don't want in life has become real within you before you actually experienced it.

Every result has a simultaneous broadcast, and it also has a source, just as you see in the examples of electricity and electronics. The entirety of what you want is found in the lamellipodia, which is the beginning point of a neuron. You want to protect this initial source of what you want, and the best way to this is, and provide the right environment, is to first structure relationships around this baby neuron. The existence of this neuron is real. It is an actual substance that represents the entirety of what you want to accomplish. To be aware and to know of this existence is crucial because the protection of your dream starts with the protection of what's in your mind. Here's a relationship chart stemming from the earlier chapters that will help you with this.

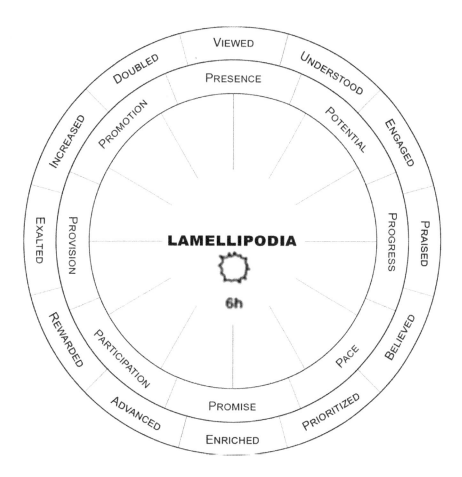

These are the energies around you that you should naturally expect the people around you to portray. Think of these as energy channels going straight to your brain that nurture the neurons. This is almost the same process as watering a seed in order for it to become what it already is.

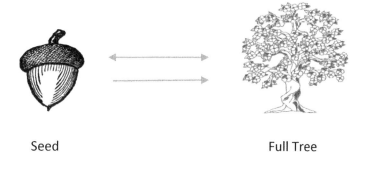

Seed   Full Tree

Action Potential

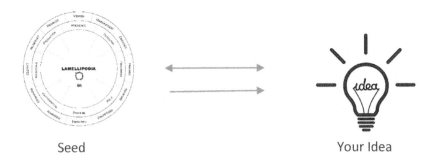

Seed   Your Idea

Action Potential (Your Choices)

So in essence, protecting and providing the right energy and environment for the initiating processes, located in your brain's neuron, is the same as providing the right energy and environment for your idea.

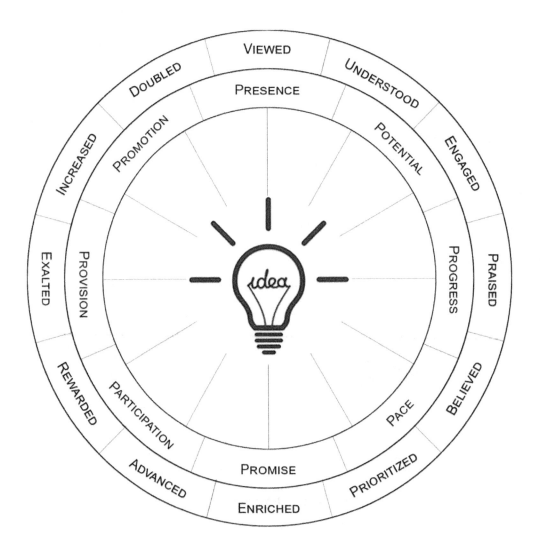

I cannot emphasize enough that "what you think is what you become", and that becoming starts with the initiating lamellipodia that end up being fully grown neurons in your brain. The accomplishment of what is in your brain, in the form of neurons, becomes imminent because that's how nature works. So you're thinking and the surrounding investments in your thinking must be guided by you and cannot be taken for granted. What you think will happen. So if it has not happened, then the environment is not right to uphold your dreams or uphold what you want to accomplish.

So let's break down the secrets of growing and knowing your completions.

1. Make a choice towards your purpose. Determine your light or idea.

    a. Choose your completions.

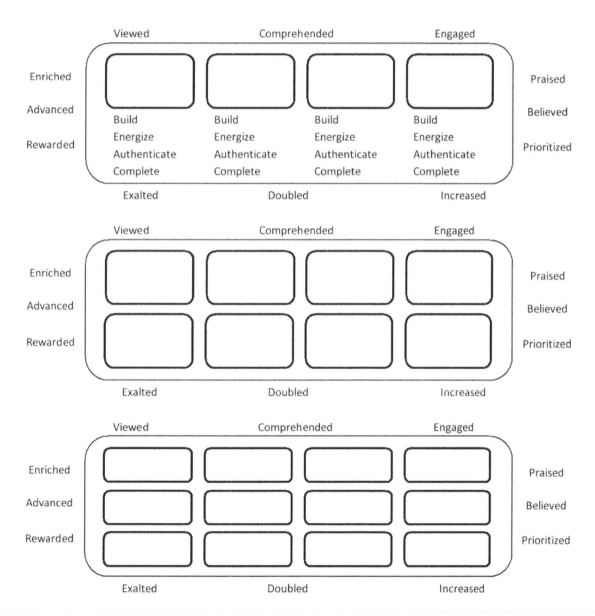

b. Know each chamber well. Build it in your body.
   c. Be aware that what you choose is already being broadcasted.
   d. Your environment affects your broadcast and your endpoints

Here you must trust the presence of what's being broadcasted from you. As I stated earlier, your dream and desire, by means of broadcast, exist in totality just because you came up with the idea. The law of action potential demands this because immediate action, starting with the splitting of water and the push of electricity initiating the lamellipodia in your brain, which eventually becomes a neuron, is responding to your thought processes. And the substance of what you want extends into your body via the responding hormones and their neurotransmitters. Literally, when you think of something, you have actually finished it before you started. Now you must use action potential, stemming from your choices, to grow what you want in life from its humble beginnings.

Trusting in What's Imminent

Here's where we go into a little bit of detail about knowing your completions. You think of something you want and you actually don't get it. It is not because it did not exist. It is because, at some point, it fell by the wayside. At some point, something else became more important than what you wanted. I have to challenge most personal development specialist out there now, when they say, failure is a part of success. The old adage goes, so if at first you don't succeed, try, try again. This is actually bad advice, because you never can get at the root of what's causing the failures. Yes, a few people will get lucky and strike the right balance point to their success, but there are millions who are trying over and over again without recognizing was really happening to the ideal of what they want to accomplish. Trying again is their   only   strategy.

What actually has to happen is that you have to trust in what's imminent. You must learn that what you want in life becomes imminent in your mind and body first. This means that the process towards your success has already begun. This process is imminent once started and energized.

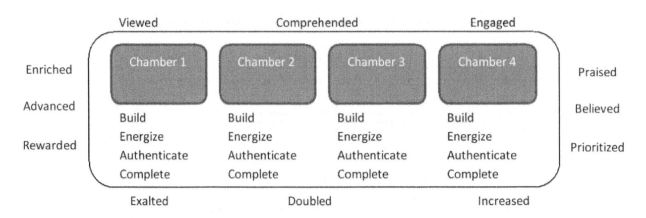

The biological process, which has already started in your body as an imminent point of development of what you decide you want in life, must now expand outside of your body in a series of actions. You must first create the relationships and an environment that is conducive to what is in your mind.

Start at the smallest common denominator. What do I mean by this? The common denominator is your end goal. What is it about your end goal that you can do now in a smaller way? Once you have documented that, no less than a few seconds after, get started. Buy the material. Make the phone call. Set the meeting. If you can't sell in the mall, sell on the street corner. Remember when you fill up or complete this initiating level, your next level will automatically be present. Remember you make the start because the chemicals in your body have already started and are there to support you with thousands to billions of years of experience.

1. List Your Starting Point

   _____

2. Date Your Starting Point (Today's Date)

   _____

3. What is Your Top Cycle or Your Planned Finishing Point

   _____

4. Start

Your Approach to Building Your Completions

Complete the same exercise when it comes to your growth. What's your level of intelligence when it comes to determining what you want to complete in life? _____

You can copy this page and use it for your completion strategies. Apply it when setting your finishing points. Know that your completions are imminent.

All Knowing	_____
Clairvoyant Constructive	_____
Innovative	_____
Creative	_____
Coordinal	_____
Advanced	_____
Basic	_____
Primal	_____

Cross out the old check and write in your new level of intelligence: _____

Write in your new language using the energy of the intelligence level you desire.

_____
_____
_____
_____

Enhancing the Process

Here are four processes to use in conjunction with the four components of this workbook that will enhance your efforts. They are as follows.

1. Hear Your Inspirations
2. Put in the Work
3. Rest in Your Work
4. Regenerate Your Success

Get Out of Your Own Way

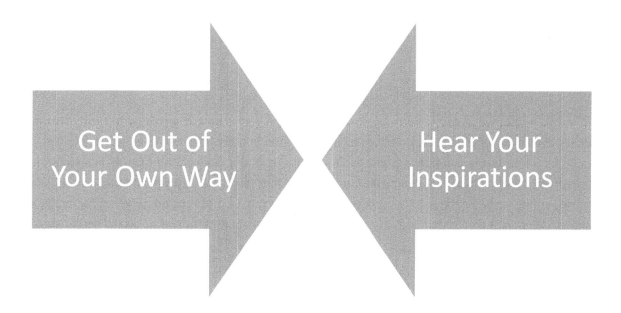

Your ability to hear your greatness involves getting out of your own way. Then you surround yourself with the 3 types of effective persons. You must let go of things that don't work and restate past circumstance to your advantage. With this, you open yourself up to hearing exactly what you want and exactly what needs to be done to obtain what you want. Be sure to stop long enough to hear your greatness.

Create Great Relationships

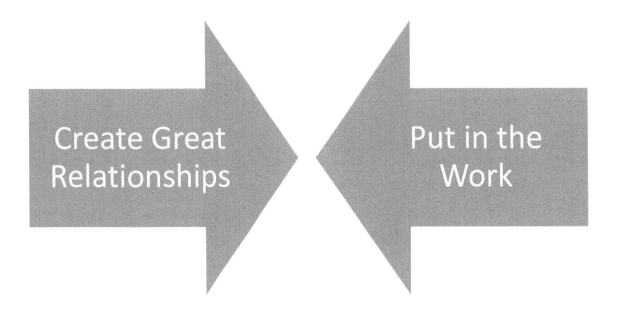

The purpose of aligning great relationships to your destiny is to create the energy to do the work that catapults you towards your goals. In order to do the work, you must have the energy to do the work. Most times when you are not energized for the work, it is because of the lack of investments and support from others. There is a chemical in your brain that flows that incites action. That chemical is called dopamine. It order for it to be active, relationships must be optimized, which affect your heart hormone ANP. When these hormones are heightened, your Action Potential is naturally heightened.

Strategies for Growth

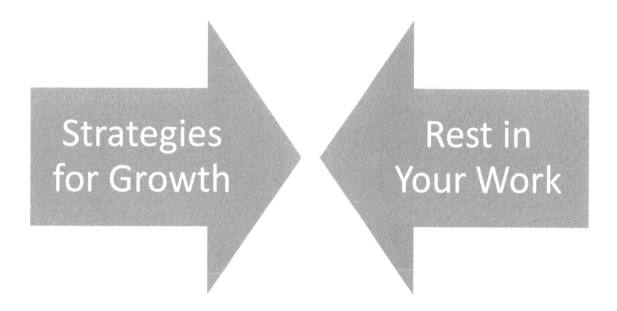

The moment you come up with an idea or something that sparks excitement, you should begin to take some type of action towards what you want. But make sure the action that you're taking is an action that can be completed. Remember, completion or the filling of one stage automatically leads to the next stage. This is led by the inspiration of what to do at the next stage. You make your move again. Stop. Take it in. Revitalize. Everything is presented back to you. You start again.

This is the basis of a concept called biofeedback. Your total existence is in a feedback loop. This is how you are alive. Biofeedback is energy presented back to you that affects the very core of the functionality of your biological systems. It involves your nervous system primarily. Remember we discussed the circadian rhythms? Your entire body is a system of rhythms, and it is functioning in the exact same way that I'm explaining to you, with regards to rest. Your body is constantly taking on new information, but what is fascinating is this new information is coming from you. Your body is learning how to live from itself. In essence, mechanisms in your body are placed to teach your body how to perform.

When you create a feedback loop of what you want to accomplish, you must remain in your loop. This is resting in your work and not being distracted by resting in the energy of somebody else's desire.

Build in Your Completions

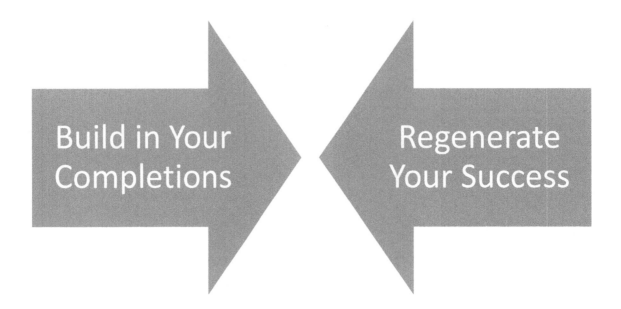

Once you master the process of moving the natural process that successfully grows your body to the process of accomplishing your dreams, you position yourself to regenerate your success at every completion point. Remember, completing one level automatically opens you up to the next level. This forces a natural process of growth.

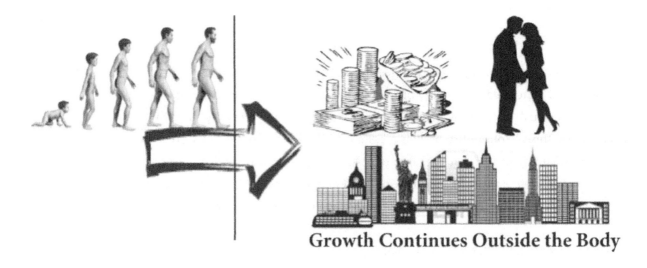

Growth Continues Outside the Body

Everything in life is meant for growth, including your personal success. You must position yourself for growth and prime yourself to start. Go over these strategies over and over until it's a natural part of who you are. Be sure that you monitor your intelligence level as you approach the exercises and strategies. Once you surround yourself, your ideas, and your purpose with correct succession of relationships, you will find yourself progressing at an astonishing pace. Enhance your surrounding environment to ensure that you maintain an effective pace towards your accomplishments.

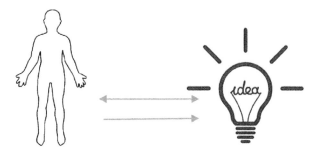

You are equivalent to your idea. Do not sell yourself short by underestimating what you can complete. There is greatness in you and that greatness is meant to live outside of you.

43611847R00060

Made in the USA
Middletown, DE
27 April 2019